Paper + Craft

Paper + Craft

25 Charming Gifts, Accents, and Accessories to Make from Paper

by Minhee & Truman Cho of Paper + Cup

With Randi Brookman Harris

Photographs by Johnny Miller

CHRONICLE BOOKS

SAN FRANCISCO

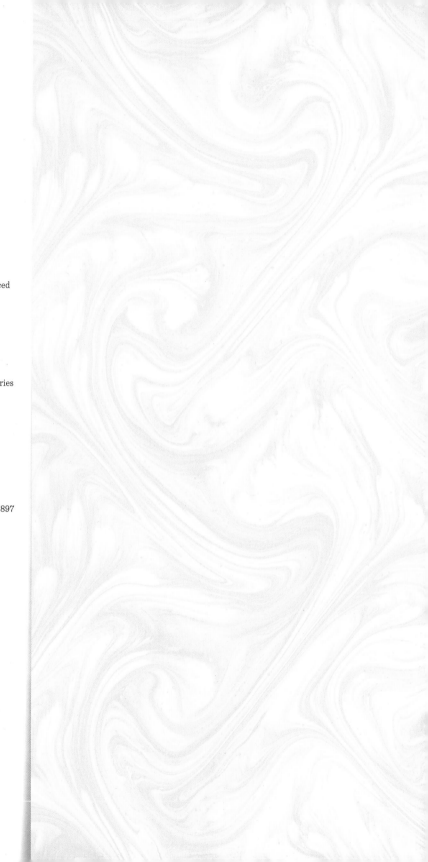

Library of Congress Cataloging-in-Publication Data:

Cho, Minhee.
    Paper + Craft : 25 charming gifts, accents, and accessories
    to make with paper / Minhee & Truman Cho.
        p. cm.

    ISBN 978-0-8118-7462-5

    1. Paper work. I. Cho, Truman. II. Title.

TT870.C492 2010
745.54—dc22

                            2009039897

Manufactured in China
Designed by Barbara Glauber/Heavy Meta
with Erika Nishizato and Rich Watts.
Styling by Randi Brookman Harris.

10 9 8 7 6 5 4 3 2 1

Chronicle Books LLC
680 Second Street
San Francisco, California 94107
www.chroniclebooks.com

CONTENTS

craft \ˈkraft, krahft\
vt : to make or manufacture (an object, objects, product, etc.) with skill and careful attention to detail

———————————◄●►———————————

By definition, all art can be considered a form of crafting, but can all crafting be considered a form of art?

Admittedly, as a stationery and design company, our initial impression of the world of "crafting" was yarn-spun doilies and Grandma's needlepoint. As noble as that is and as much skill as it takes to accomplish these traditional crafts, that just didn't quite appeal to our artistic sensibilities. However, upon reading the definition of the word *craft*, we were shocked to realize that our day-to-day existence was built around exactly that: the making or manufacturing of an object with skill and careful attention to detail. In the time that it took to read that definition, we had gone from feeling slightly superior to the craft world to joining in it, proudly considering ourselves "crafters" for the first time.

Crafting is a deeply meaningful experience due to the pride we feel in creating something tangible. Crafts express our taste and personality in a tactile way, and are the physical result of the time and creativity that goes into a project. If we give a craft as a gift, it conveys a unique sentiment and personality to the receiver. For instance, when we give presents to loved ones, it is customary to include a card or note to express our affection. When we take the time to write that simple greeting, we are in fact *crafting* a letter as a small extension of our affections. It elevates the meaning of an otherwise inanimate object.

Crafting with paper is a natural extension of our fondness for the medium. We love paper for its accessibility and for the limitless possibilities that a blank sheet offers us. It is the literal and modern version of "starting with a clean slate."

It was, in fact, the need for a new beginning in late 2003 that inspired us to start Paper+Cup Design. With backgrounds in graphic design and an avid interest in paper products, we had always wanted to collaborate on something of our own that would satisfy our urge to express our creativity. When Minhee made the decision to start anew and quit her job as an art director, the slate was officially cleaned. Sure enough, just like staring at a blank sheet of paper, there was a familiar weight of intimidation with a healthy dose of optimism as well. So many possibilities! Once the initial terror of starting our own business subsided, we turned to the most convenient and available material within our reach—paper—and began to create different types of products. Within months, the debut stationery collection of Paper+Cup Design was completed, and our business was born. Today, we are a design company that specializes in graphic design, social stationery, and custom invitations, with a design philosophy rooted in the idea that "Everyone has a story." Whether it is creating a brand identity for a company or business, or putting together birthday invitations for six-year-olds, there is always a story to convey and celebrate through our paper products.

Building on this idea, we wanted to write a paper-crafting book to demonstrate the ways we approach projects and stretch our creativity in order to connect with the world around us. Our goal is to bring you the insight and pleasure we have gained from embracing our crafty side through a medium we love, and to introduce a lesser-known, contemporary way of crafting.

The projects in this book are easy to make whether you are a seasoned crafter or beginner. We hope you undertake them in a spirit of inspiration rather than mimicry. The allure of crafting is that it fills the mundane with substance, and regardless of the imperfections or irregularities that will happen along the way, it is still entirely "yours," no matter how simple the object. Most important, always remember that as long as you are creating something with skill and attention to detail, congratulations—you are a crafter!

MINHEE & TRUMAN CHO
Paper+Cup Design

How to Use This Book

In this book, you'll find twenty-five projects that explore the many different techniques and methods of paper crafting.

Many of the projects leave room for your own interpretations and variations. Once you learn the basic techniques, there are endless ways to mix and match the instructions here to create your own paper crafts.

Each project has an introduction describing our inspiration for the piece, as well as a full list of supplies needed to make the craft. We've provided step-by-step instructions and how-to illustrations to further explain the techniques. Some items require templates, which you can easily download from www.chroniclebooks.com/papercraft and print out.

Materials

Before you start a project, please refer to the back of the book to familiarize yourself with the Materials, Tools & Resources section. This may save you time and multiple trips to the art store. Since all of the projects are paper oriented, it is a good idea to stock up on the following basic tools and supplies:

ADHESIVE: Most projects require some sort of adhering method. Glue stick, craft glue, and double-sided tape are great to have on hand to give you a variety of options, depending on the project.

CRAFT HOLE PUNCHES (VARIOUS): Not mandatory tools, but always good to have around for embellishing.

CUTTING MAT: Most projects require cutting and pasting, so we highly recommend investing in this self-healing mat. It will protect your work surface and help you get clean cuts when using with a metal ruler and utility knife.

PAPER: Keep a variety of colored and patterned paper in various weights, from cover to text weight (see the Materials section in the back of the book for paper-weight explanations). It is also a good idea to have cards that are presized and cut, such as squares, circles, and folded cards. Having a ready supply of goods will save you many trips to the stationery/art store!

PENCILS AND ERASERS: No. 2 pencils work just fine for these projects. Keep a good rubber eraser and pencil sharpener handy.

RULERS: Necessary for getting nice, straight cuts. We recommend a cord-backed metal ruler and triangle.

SCISSORS: Keep these handy for cutting and trimming.

UTILITY KNIFE: An essential tool for cutting clean, crisp edges. Be sure to replace the blades often.

Projects

FLAG
Banner

Party banners are classic, and constructing one is a quick and effective way to brighten up any event. You can keep it simple with bold patterns or go all-out to create a very detailed and intricate sign. You may even want to try turning this into a group project. Kids, friends, and relatives can join in to create a memorable keepsake for the honoree to hold on to. For an added surprise have everyone sign their names and write a congratulatory note on the back of each flag.

Supplies

Tape measure

1 sheet 8½-by-11-in
(22-by-28-cm) plain
cover-weight paper

Pencil

Ruler or metal straightedge

Utility knife with ⅛-in
(3-mm) blade (plus spare
blades)

Cutting mat

Patterned and solid-color
paper. Amount will vary
depending on length
of banner. One 8½-by-
11-in (22-by-28-cm)
sheet makes two 6-in
(15.2-cm) triangles.

¼-in (6-mm) hole punch

¼-in-wide (6-mm) ribbon

❶ Determine the length of the banner.

Using a tape measure, determine how long the banner needs to be. (The length of ribbon used for the banner will need to equal this measurement.) If the banner will be made up of words, count the number of letters in your message. For example, "Happy Birthday" requires 13 letters, plus a triangle for the space in between the words (see Fig. 1). *Hint*: Divide the length of the flag-hanging area by the number of letters in the banner. This way you will know approximately how wide the top edge of each triangle should be.

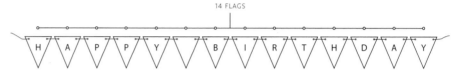

Fig. 1

❷ Draw the triangle template.

Take a piece of plain cover-weight paper and use the top edge as the top of the triangle template. Using a pencil and ruler, mark the width of the triangle. In our example, we made the top edge of the triangle 6 in (15 cm) wide. Find the center (ours was 3 in [7.5 cm] across), and mark with a pencil. Decide how long the triangle should be (we made ours 6 in, or 15 cm, tall). From the center mark, draw a vertical line that is the length you have chosen and connect the lines from each corner, creating the triangle (see Fig. 2).

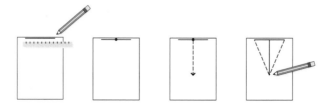

Fig. 2

③ Cut out the template.

Using a utility knife and ruler, carefully cut out the finished triangle template on a cutting mat (see Fig. 3).

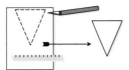

Fig. 3

④ Form the flags.

Lay the template on the back side of the paper you will use for the triangles in the banner. Using a pencil, trace the template shape onto the paper. Repeat until you have the number of triangles you will need for the banner. Using a utility knife and ruler, carefully cut out all the triangles on a cutting mat (see Fig. 4).

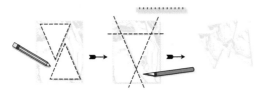

Fig. 4

Continued...

⑤ Finishing touches.

Using a hole punch, make a hole near the two top corners of each flag (see Fig. 5). Thread the ribbon through the holes in each flag (see Fig. 6). Hang the banner.

Fig. 5   *Fig. 6*

Additional Ideas

....

Experiment with other shapes, like circles and squares, for a different look.

....

Use stencils to paint letters onto the flags, or cut them out and paste on with glue.

....

Print out your favorite photos and attach them to the flags. This makes a fun anniversary or birthday banner.

....

For extra color, add ribbon strips between each flag after they are strung together.

giant FLOWER in vase

Nothing really compares to fresh flowers when it comes to brightening up a room, but this imaginative paper craft is a great alternative. Not only is it inexpensive to create, but it lasts longer and is much easier to maintain! This flower can be used for anything from accenting a living room to embellishing the umbrella holder in your foyer. In our small apartment in Brooklyn, we situated it in a particularly dim corner near an old, unsightly radiator. It distracts the eye away from the heater and is able to withstand the extreme changes in temperature. Real flowers wouldn't stand a chance in those conditions. While silk flowers could serve the same purpose, there is something satisfying about crafting this flower on your own out of paper. Best of all, you don't have to water it.

Supplies

Flower template

3 sheets 8½-by-11-in (22-by-28-cm) plain text-weight paper

Scissors

Pencil

2 sheets 10-by-49-in (25-by-125-cm) doublette (double-thick) yellow and white crepe paper

1 sheet 20-by-96-in (50-by-250-cm) of each white, yellow, and black crepe paper

Ruler

Vase

Wire cutters

¼-in (6-mm) metal threaded rod

Paper-covered floral wire

Floral tape

1 sheet 20-by-96-in (50-by-250-cm) green crepe paper

Glue or transparent tape

❶ Cut out the flower petals.

Download the flower template from www.chroniclebooks.com/papercraft and print out onto text-weight paper. Using scissors, cut out the pieces. Then with a pencil, trace five 6-in (15-cm) and five 8-in (20-cm) petals onto the doublette yellow and white crepe paper, and five 5-in (13-cm) petals onto the white crepe paper, and five 7-in (18-cm) petals onto the yellow crepe paper (see Fig. 1).

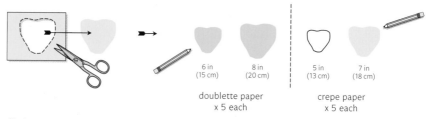

Fig. 1

❷ Make the stem.

Using a ruler, measure the height of the vase in order to determine the length of the stem. You'll want the stem to extend beyond the lip of the vase by ½ to ⅔ the height of the vase. With wire cutters, cut the thin metal rod (see Fig. 2).

Fig. 2

3 Form the flower bud.

Crumple up some of the leftover yellow crepe paper into a ball and wrap a new sheet of black crepe paper around it to form a 2½-in (6-cm)-round "bud." With scissors, cut a strip of black crepe paper that is 32 in (81 cm) long by 4 in (10 cm) wide and create a fringe by making crosswise cuts in the strip about ½ in (13 mm) apart, stopping just short of the edge so it stays intact (see Fig. 3). Starting from one edge of the fringe strip, roll it around the bud, keeping the bottom of the bud tightly pinched. Twist the ends of the bud fringes with lightly wet fingertips.

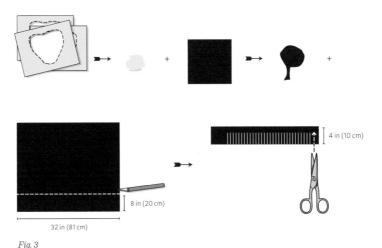

Fig. 3

Continued…

④ Add the petals to the flower.

Take the bud and place it next to the stem. Attach the pieces together by securing first with floral wire and then covering with floral tape (see Fig. 4). Then add the small white petals, placing their bases around the top of the stem, and securing with floral tape by wrapping the tape around the stem. Next, place the 6-in (15-cm) doublette yellow and white petals around the center bud, on top of the smaller petals. Secure with more floral tape by wrapping the tape around the stem (see Fig. 5). Repeat with the larger petals as you progress, until the flower has the shape you desire. Wrap the bottom of the flower and the stem with floral tape to keep the flower petals secure (see Fig. 6).

Fig. 4   Fig. 5   Fig. 6

⑤ Finishing touches.

Wrap the stem tightly with a long strip of green crepe paper to cover up the floral tape, and glue in place at the end of the stem. Place in the vase (see Fig. 7).

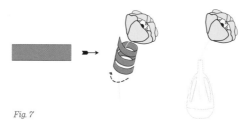

Fig. 7

Additional Ideas

···

Experiment with different shapes and sizes.
These work great for centerpieces
and boutonnieres. You can also create
an arrangement of different flowers.

···

These paper flowers can also be hung from the
ceiling for party decorations.

Birdie
MOBILE

This whimsical birdie mobile is wonderfully versatile. Use it as an understated floating centerpiece for your next dinner party; the black-and-white color scheme and delicate design allow you to dress the party up or down, depending on the occasion. Or secure it over a baby's crib as a lovely accent to the nursery. Babies will be fascinated by the birdies "flying" above.

Supplies

Bird template

1 sheet 8½-by-11-in (22-by-28-cm) cover-weight paper in any color, for template

Utility knife

Cutting mat

Pencil

2 sheets 8½-by-11-in (22-by-28-cm) cream cover-weight paper

2 sheets 8½-by-11-in (22-by-28-cm) black cover-weight paper

Newspaper (optional)

Glue stick

Needle

Three ⅟₃₂-by-12-in (1-by-305-mm) brass rods

Wire cutters

Round-nose pliers

Scissors

1 roll of string, thread, wax thread, thin ribbon, or fishing wire

❶ Make the bird templates.

Download the bird template from www.chroniclebooks.com/papercraft and print onto cover-weight paper. Using a utility knife, carefully cut out the shapes on a cutting mat (see Fig. 1). (If your printer does not accommodate the cover-weight paper, print the template on a regular sheet and cut out the birds, then trace the birds onto the cover-weight paper and cut them out to make the templates.)

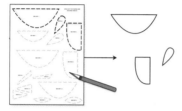

Fig. 1

❷ Cut out the birds.

Using a pencil, trace the bird-body templates onto the desired colored papers. For our samples shown, we used Birds 1, 2, and 3 on cream paper, and Bird 4 on black paper. Using a utility knife, carefully cut out the shapes on the cutting mat. Using newspaper or whatever type of paper you like for the rest of the bird pieces, trace the wings and belly elements. Cut out the shapes (see Fig. 2).

Fig. 2

❸ Assemble the birds.

Using a glue stick, attach the wings and feathers to the bird bodies. Then use a needle to make a small hole in the wing (see Fig. 3).

Fig. 3

❹ Make the mobile.

Keep one rod as is. Take one of the rods and cut it in half with the wire cutters. Take another rod and, using the wire cutters, cut a piece approximately two-thirds of the total length to give you one longer rod and one shorter rod. You won't need to use all of the rods; disregard the extra rods (or keep them for later). Then take all the rods and, using round-nose pliers, loop each end into a small, round curl: Start by pinching the very end of each rod and then slowly rotate the pliers down to curl the end inward (see Fig. 4). The long rod will be the base from which the other elements will hang.

Fig. 4

❺ Hang the birds.

With scissors, cut six pieces of string in various lengths. Thread the end of each length into the needle hole in each bird, and make a small knot so the bird hangs at the end (see Fig. 5).

Fig. 5

Continued...

6 **Finishing touches.**

Tie the other end of each length to the rods. Place the string through the loop in the rod and adjust the length. This step will require some time and experimentation. Start with the longest rod and hang the other smaller rods with the birds from it. Adjust the placement until you get the balance you like. Hang the mobile from the ceiling with more string (see Fig. 6).

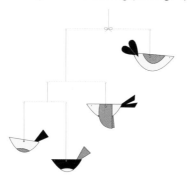

Fig. 6

Additional Ideas

Make the birds colorful instead of black-and-white. Using two strong colors, such as blue and orange or red and pink, contrasting with or complementing each other, works well.

Photographs make great mobiles, too. Assemble some of your favorites to create a story. Make them double-sided so the pictures can be seen from all sides as the mobile moves.

Play with different arrangements for the mobile by adding and subtracting rods and strings.

Make the mobile very full, with the birds clustered together, to create a chandelier effect.

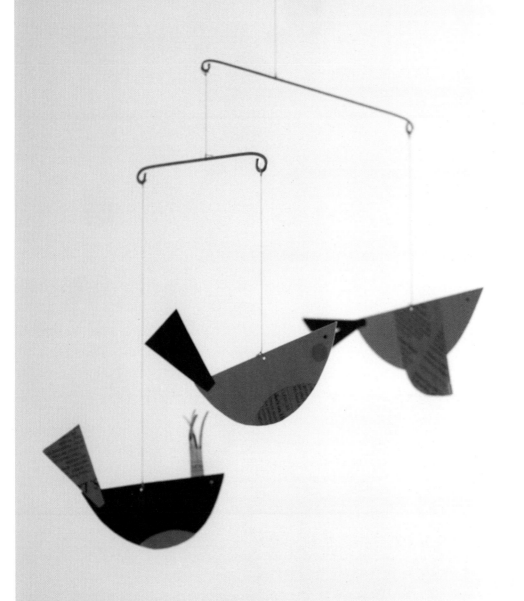

custom
SILHOUETTE

The word *silhouette* actually used to be an offensive term, named after Louis the XV's minister of finance, Étienne de Silhouette, who was infamously vilified as a penny-pinching miser. Lower-class citizens were unable to afford full-color portraits, and so instead commissioned "shade portraits," which we know today as "silhouettes." At Paper+Cup we have always been enamored of silhouettes for their quaint history and timeless charm. Known for our offbeat whims, however, we just can't let well enough alone, and have added simple twists to this timeless classic, such as using bright and colorful patterns instead of the standard black, or displaying additional cutouts of objects. These silhouettes make great gifts, and having a loved one's framed silhouette in place of a photo on your wall or office desk is enchanting.

Supplies

1 piece 8½-by-11-in
(22-by-28-cm)
photo-printing paper

Photocopier

Utility knife

Cutting mat

1 sheet 8½-by-11-in
(22-by-28-cm) black
construction or
cover-weight paper

Glass from picture frame

1 sheet chipboard

Pencil

1 sheet 8½-by-11-in
(22-by-28-cm) patterned
paper, such as wallpaper or
wrapping paper

Glue stick

Plate hanger (1 set)

① Make the silhouette.

Take a photograph of the subject's profile. (*Hint*: Place your subject in front of a plain background when taking the photo so it will be easier to trace the silhouette.) Print the photograph. Use a photocopier to adjust the size of the image if needed (see Fig. 1). With a utility knife, carefully cut out the profile on a cutting mat (see Fig. 2). This is your silhouette template.

Fig. 1

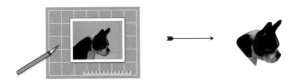

Fig. 2

② Prep the frame.

Lay black construction paper on the cutting mat. Place the glass from a picture frame on top of the black paper and, using the utility knife, cut the black paper to fit the glass. Do the same with the chipboard (see Fig. 3).

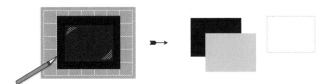

Fig. 3

③ Construct the silhouette.

Using a pencil, trace the silhouette template onto the back side of the patterned paper. With a utility knife, carefully cut out the silhouette on the cutting mat. Position the silhouette, pattern-side up, on the black paper and lightly mark with pencil where it should be placed (see Fig. 4). Apply glue all over the back side of the silhouette and paste the silhouette onto the black paper (see Fig. 5).

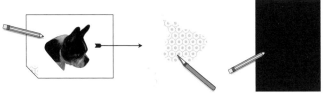

Fig. 4

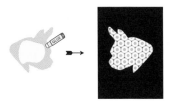

Fig. 5

Continued...

4 Finishing touches.

Place the black paper on top of the chipboard. Place the glass on top and secure with the plate hanger. Hang on the wall (see Fig. 6).

Fig. 6

Additional Ideas

Make a wall of silhouettes in various sizes and frames. Found vintage frames add charm. Or keep it sleek and modern, using different sizes of the same frame type.

Experiment with different colored and patterned papers, such as vintage wallpaper, wrapping paper, brown Kraft paper, and magazine pages.

Monogrammed

NIGHT-LIGHT

A monogrammed night-light is a great project for parents to share with their little ones. The best part about this easy-to-do craft is that, aside from livening up a child's bedroom with his or her own personal touch, it can be a fantastic way to entice children into sleeping alone in their own room. The more involved children are in putting their little creative stamps on the project, the more excited they will be in anticipating the outcome. Come to think of it, isn't this exactly what makes crafting fun for adults as well? Of course, this project isn't *only* for kids. You can monogram the initial of your last name and hang the night-light in the bathroom or hallway, or make one for a friend.

Supplies

1 sheet 8½-by-11-in (22-by-28-cm) patterned paper

Night-light with half lampshade

Pencil

Scissors

Monogram template

1 sheet 8½-by-11-in (22-by-28-cm) paper for the monogram in a dark shade such as black, gray, or brown

Photocopier, for adjusting monogram size (optional)

Utility knife

Ruler

Cutting mat

Pinking scissors

Glue stick

① Create the shade cover.

Place a patterned paper for the night-light cover facedown on a clean work surface. Remove the night-light shade and, using a pencil, slowly trace the shade shape onto the paper. Start at one side of the shade and roll it along the paper, following the edge with the pencil. You can also try wrapping the paper around the shade with one hand and tracing around it with the other. Using scissors, cut out the shape of the shade (see Fig. 1).

Fig. 1

② Create the monogram cutout.

Download a monogram template from www.chroniclebooks.com/papercraft and print onto your desired colored paper. Size it to fit the shade cover using a photocopier, if needed. Using a utility knife and ruler (to achieve sharp, clean lines), carefully cut out your letter on a cutting mat (see Fig. 2).

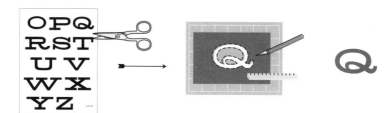

Fig. 2

③ Decorate the paper shade.

To create the rickracking shown in the photograph, take the same paper used for your monogram and trace the bottom of the night-light shade. Using a pencil, mark about ½ in (13 mm) up from the tracing line and cut it out, using pinking scissors for the bottom of the trim and regular scissors for the rest (see Fig. 3). Position the rickrack trim at the bottom of the shade to make sure it fits. Apply some glue with a glue stick to only the top edge of the trim and attach to the base of the night-light shade (see Fig. 4). Apply some glue onto the backside of the shade cover, then take the shade cover and place it on top of the night-light cover. Smooth it out with your fingers and make sure it is well attached. Position the letter in the center of the shade and apply a small amount of glue to the back of the letter. Adhere to the center of the shade (see Fig. 5).

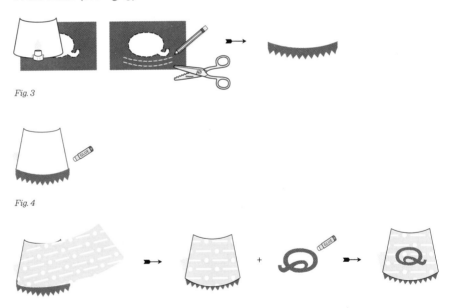

Fig. 3

Fig. 4

Fig. 5

Continued...

4 Finishing touches.

Attach the shade cover to the light and plug the finished night-light into the wall (see Fig. 6).

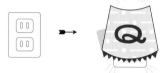

Fig. 6

Additional Ideas

Use fun childhood icons like trains, boats, airplanes, flowers, and stars in place of letters. These can be found in clip-art books from the bookstore.

More advanced crafters may choose to let the child receiving the shade choose his or her favorite superhero logo and superimpose a personal monogram onto the design.

Pinwheel NAME CARDS

When attending different functions or dinner parties, we like to have little tokens of the event to keep as a reminder of the occasion. This must stem from our infatuation with paper, but we have always had a habit of holding on to branded cocktail napkins, party favors, and sometimes even handwritten name cards. When we host parties or gatherings, we like to provide guests with fun little knickknacks that can double as place cards. These pinwheel name cards are perfect for events such as children's birthday parties, barbecues, or picnics. We find that they give guests a colorful accessory and keep their hands occupied while they get over their initial bashfulness in larger groups. We defy anyone to pick one up without giving it a maiden spin.

Supplies

Scissors

8½-by-11-in (22-by-28-cm) cover-weight paper in various colors and patterns (1 sheet makes two 5-in [12.7-cm] pinwheels; lighter-weight, not too stiff paper works best)

Pushpin

Pencil

Ruler

Utility knife

Cutting mat

Round-head pins at least 1 in (2.5 cm) in length

Acrylic paint for dowels (optional)

12-in (30.5-cm)-long wooden dowels

¼-in (6-mm) hole punch

Chipboard in small scraps, about 4 in by 4 in (10 cm by 10 cm)

Hot glue gun

Metal rim tags in choice of color

Marker or fine-point pen

⅛-in (3-mm)-wide ribbon or string

Dried moss

Floral foam

Bowls

① Prep the pinwheel sheets.

Using scissors, cut the cover-weight paper into squares in the size you want for your pinwheels. We used a 3-in (7.5-cm) and a 5-in (12-cm) square. Find the center of each square and mark it with a pushpin, creating a small hole (see Fig. 1).

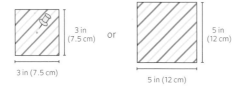

Fig. 1

② Cut the pinwheel sheets.

On a work surface, lay your paper square with the pattern side down, and use a pencil and ruler to draw a diagonal line from each corner to make an X. With a utility knife and a cutting mat, carefully cut along the diagonal lines. Stop cutting before you reach the hole in the center. (For our 5-in [12-cm] square, we stopped 1 in [2.5 cm] from the center; for the 3-in [7.5 cm] square, we stopped ¾ in [2 cm]; see Fig. 2.)

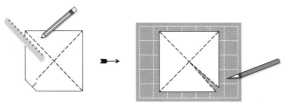

Fig. 2

③ Form the pinwheel.

Lay the square on your work surface, patterned-side up. Use the pushpin to make a hole in the right-hand corner of each section of the square (see Fig. 3). Flip the square over so the patterned side is facing down. One by one, bring each of the four holed corners to the center with the corners overlapping each other (see Fig. 4), and stick a round-head pin through all of the four holes from the front.

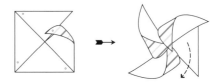

Fig. 3   *Fig. 4*

④ Prep the dowel.

Paint the dowels, if desired, and let dry. Use the pushpin to make a hole on the dowel, ½ in (13 mm) from the top (see Fig. 5). Using a hole punch, punch two holes through the chipboard (see Fig. 6), saving the round punched pieces. (These will be used for extra backing when putting the pinwheel together.) Set aside.

Fig. 5   *Fig. 6*

⑤ Assemble all the parts.

Take the assembled pinwheel head and both of the round punched chipboard pieces. Insert the punched piece onto the round-head pin that is holding the pinwheel head together, through the center at the back of the pinwheel head. Slide the round punched piece close to the pinwheel so it fits pretty snugly together. This will allow the pinwheel to spin around. Put a drop of hot glue in the hole in the dowel and quickly insert the pin running through the pinwheel head into the hole on the dowel (see Fig. 7). Be careful not to let the pinwheel paper or the round punched piece touch the glue on the dowel while it's drying. If it sticks, it won't be able to spin. Repeat steps 1 through 5 until you have one pinwheel for each guest.

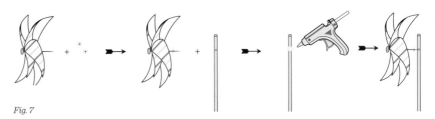

Fig. 7

Continued…

⑥ Make the name tags.

Use the metal rim tags to create the name tags. With a marker, write the name of a guest on the front and his or her table number on the back (see Fig. 8).

Fig. 8

⑦ Attach the name tags to the pinwheels.

Cut a small strip of ribbon and insert it into the hole of the metal rim tag. Tie it around the dowel in a tight knot (see Fig. 9). Repeat until all of the pinwheels are identified with name tags.

Fig. 9

⑧ Finishing touches.

Place a bed of moss atop a chunk of wet floral foam in a little bowl. Stick each dowel firmly into the foam through the moss. Display on a table. Now your guests can find their names and enjoy their pinwheels!

Additional Ideas

Try different pinwheel shapes. Cut wavy lines to create a floral look or use scalloped or patterned scissors for an interesting edge.

Use paper punches for the centers.

Scan vintage patterns or favorite illustrations for a custom look.

flower
headpiece

These tissue-flower headpieces make a stunning fashion statement and are different from all of the other flower hair clips out there. Wear this out on the town, or craft one to give to the guest of honor at a birthday party or celebration. It sure beats a paper party hat!

Supplies

Scissors

4 sheets 8-by-12-in
(20-by-30-cm) tissue paper
in desired colors

2 sheets 20-by-96-in
(50-by-250-cm) crepe
paper in desired colors

Pencil

Needle

Thread in color that
coordinates with
or matches tissue and
crepe paper

Hot glue gun or fabric glue

Hair comb, bobby pin,
or fabric hairband

❶ Prep the tissue flower.

Using scissors, cut 20 square sheets from the tissue and crepe paper. The size of the squares will depend on the size of the flower you wish to make. The flower in the photograph is about 10 in (25 cm) in size. Use a variety of papers to give the flower some texture. Stack the squares, alternating the papers and colors. Using a pencil, lightly draw a flower shape on the top sheet and cut out through all the sheets (see Fig. 1). A loosely drawn petal shape works best.

Fig. 1

❷ Assemble the flower.

Stack the flowers together and fold in half. Fold in half again (see Fig. 2).

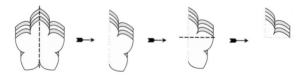

Fig. 2

❸ Create the flower.

Using a needle and thread, sew 3 or 4 stitches along the folded edge. Gently open the flower and fluff the petals (see Fig. 3).

Fig. 3

4 **Add the flower to the headpiece.**

Apply a few drops of glue to the comb. Add the flower and hold in position until set (see Fig. 4).

Fig. 4

Additional Ideas

....

Add leaves to the headpiece.

....

Add a strip of paper and write the name of the person, or "The Bride," "Birthday Girl," or another fun title.

....

More can be better! Add flowers in various sizes and shapes to create a glorious crown. Keep it all one hue, or go all out and use a rainbow of colors.

....

Add a long ribbon to create a flowing look.

wrapped
CANDLE
HOLDER

This project is a great way to celebrate your fondest memories and can also serve as an expressive gift. Use paper mementos, such as ticket stubs or photos, or choose pretty patterned paper to wrap the glass jar for your candle holder. Regardless of the paper products you use, these decorative candle holders look wonderful displayed on mantelpieces, dressers, and nightstands.

Supplies

Tape measure

Glass jar in any size, preferably with a smooth surface

Various kinds of paper and ephemera, such as scraps of wrapping paper, photocopies of old letters, mementos, or photos

Photocopier

1 sheet 11-by-17-in (28-by-43-cm) text-weight paper in white

Ruler

Pencil

Utility knife

Cutting mat

Glue stick

Candle to fit inside jar

Matches

① Cut out the template and prepare the paper.

Using a tape measure, measure the height and width of the jar that is to be covered, adding an extra 1 in (2.5 cm) to the width (see Fig. 1). Prep the ephemera by making color photocopies onto text-weight paper (see Fig. 2).

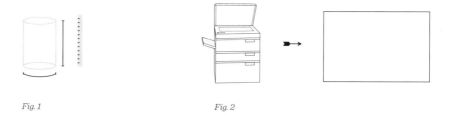

Fig. 1   *Fig. 2*

② Fit the paper around the jar.

Using a ruler and pencil, draw a rectangle in the dimensions determined in step 1 onto the strip of printed ephemera or patterned paper. Carefully cut out with a utility knife on a cutting mat. Wrap the paper around the jar to make sure it fits, with a bit of overlap (see Fig. 3).

Fig. 3

③ Wrap the jar.

Apply glue to one edge of the back side of the jar wrap, and wrap around the glass jar (see Fig. 4). Overlap the wrap ends and press to seal. Insert a candle and light (see Fig. 5).

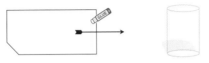

Fig. 4

Fig. 5

Additional Ideas

For a quick fix, try ready-made paper found in scrapbooking stores, wrapping paper, or even just pretty colored tissue.

Use transparent vellum paper with punches in different shapes for a simple, modern look.

FLOWER GIFT TAG

Flowers brighten anyone's day—especially when paired with a gift. These darling flower gift tags are simple to make and add an unforgettable accent that the recipient can keep or reuse. In addition to serving as pretty tags, these flowers can also be used as place settings or corsages.

Supplies

Scissors

1 sheet 10-by-49-in
(25-by-125-cm)
doublette (double-thick)
crepe paper in desired
color

Glue stick

1 sheet 8½-by-11-in
(22-by-28-cm) green
cover-weight paper

28-gauge floral wire

Green floral tape
(wire glue tape)

Pencil

Pen

Ribbon (optional)

Hot glue (optional)

1 Prep the flower.

Using scissors, cut a 25-by-4-in (63.5-by-10 cm) strip from the crepe paper
(see Fig. 1).

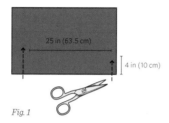

25 in (63.5 cm)

4 in (10 cm)

Fig. 1

2 Form the flower shape.

Fold the strip in half crosswise three times. Using scissors, create a fringe by cutting ¼-in (6-mm) strips along one edge, stopping ½ inch (13 mm) short of the other
edge (see Fig. 2). Then, create small arch-shaped petals out of the fringed pieces
with scissors (see Fig. 3).

Fig. 2

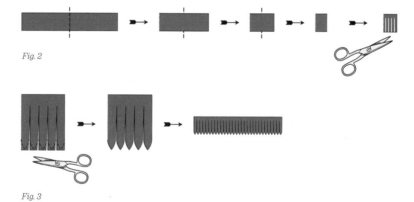

Fig. 3

③ Finish up the flower.

While holding on to the edge of the strip (the base) with your left hand, with your right hand start wrapping the strip in a tight coil, forming a center. Use glue as you wrap to keep the pieces tight and intact. Continue to keep the base pinched with your fingers. When there is about 2 in (5 cm) left of the crepe paper, fold the rest to create a little stem (see Fig. 4). Do this by continuing to wrap the crepe paper but instead of keeping it pinched at the base, wrap down the base to create a thin strip that can serve as a stem.

Fig. 4

④ Make the leaves.

Cut two 3-in (7.5-cm)-square sheets from the green cover-weight paper. Cut a 4-in (10-cm) length of floral wire and lay it so that 1 in (2.5 cm) of the end of the wire is atop one of the green sheets. Apply glue to the other green sheet and attach so the wire is sandwiched in between (see Fig. 5). Using scissors, cut a leaf shape out of the sandwiched green cover-weight paper, leaving the wire to stick out as the stem (see Fig. 6).

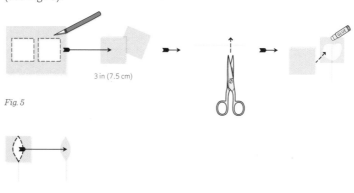

3 in (7.5 cm)

Fig. 5

Fig. 6

Continued…

⑤ Finishing touches.

Align the wire stem with the paper stem from the flower base. Get the wire as close to the base of the flower as possible. Wrap the wire around the flower to create the rest of the flower stem. Use the green floral tape to wrap the base of the flower and stem. Using a pencil, curl the flower strips gently for a fluffier look. With a pen, write the name of the recipient on the leaf (see Fig. 7). Add to the wrapped gift look by tying ribbon around the stem and then finishing with a bow, if desired. Or attach the flower gift tag to a present with a dab of hot glue.

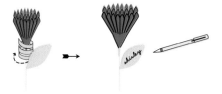

Fig. 7

Additional Ideas

....

Tissue paper works well, too. Use decorative-edge scissors to create a different texture. You can use the same method and play with different edges, creating unique looks for each flower.

....

Add more than one flower, making a smaller, budlike flower and extra leaves.

....

Attach pins to the back of flowers with a hot glue gun so guests can wear them like boutonnieres.

....

Make a flower corsage by extending the ribbon. Wear it on your wrist.

keepsake
PAPER
BOX

This paper box can be used to store your favorite keepsakes. We've given it a travel theme; construct this box after a memorable trip and fill it with any tickets, notes, or ephemera you picked up along the way. It also makes a great gift for someone who is embarking on a journey, or has just returned from one. Feel free to opt out of the travel theme if you like, and give it your own personal spin.

Supplies

Box templates

Map template

Vintage label template

2 sheets 11-by-17-in (28-by-43-cm) plain text-weight paper

One 8½-by-11-in (22-by-280-cm) sheet white labels

2 sheets 11-by-17-in (28-by-43 cm) cream cover-weight paper

Double-sided tape

Utility knife

Ruler

Cutting mat

Bone folder

Glue stick

Scissors

1 sheet 8½-by-11-in (22-by-28-cm) lighter-weight paper for the map

❶ Create the templates.

Download the box, map (of your choice), and vintage label templates from www.chroniclebooks.com/papercraft. Print out the box templates onto the plain text-weight paper. There are two template pieces: one for the lid and one for the bottom of the box. (For larger boxes, you can tile the template when printing.) Print out the map template onto lighter-weight paper. Print out the vintage label onto the white label sheet.

❷ Cut out the box templates.

Place the printed double-sided template on top of the cover-weight paper. Apply tape to keep it in place. Adhere it along the spaces that will be cut out, not on the actual box template (see Fig. 1).

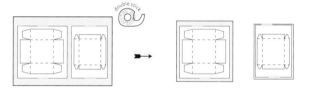

Fig. 1

❸ Score the box.

Using a utility knife and ruler, carefully cut along the template lines on a cutting mat. Using the bone folder and ruler, score along the dotted lines within the template. With your fingers, gently fold along the scored lines. Do this for both of the box pieces (see Fig. 2).

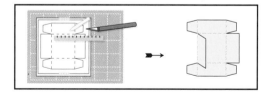

Fig. 2

❹ Finalize the box construction.

Fold up the box so you can see where the flaps need to be glued down. Apply glue stick to the flaps and glue down in the appropriate places, gently creasing the edges with your fingers so they bend at 90 degrees. Repeat on all sides until both of the box pieces are finished (see Fig. 3).

Fig. 3

❺ Finishing touches.

The finished box can be used for storage or as a gift, but our favorite use is as a travel/memento box. Cut out the map template with scissors and trace onto desired paper. We used a map wrapping paper, but any lighter-weight paper will do. Cut out the shape with scissors and apply it to the lid of the box with a glue stick (see Fig. 4). Cut out the label pieces and adorn your box however you want. Fill the box with contents from your travels.

Fig. 4

Additional Ideas

For a modern look, cut out letters and decoupage them onto the box, or use stencils.

Attach a favorite photo to the lid.

These boxes can make great gifts. Decoupage the name or a photo of your recipient on the cover. Tie it with a bow for a finishing touch.

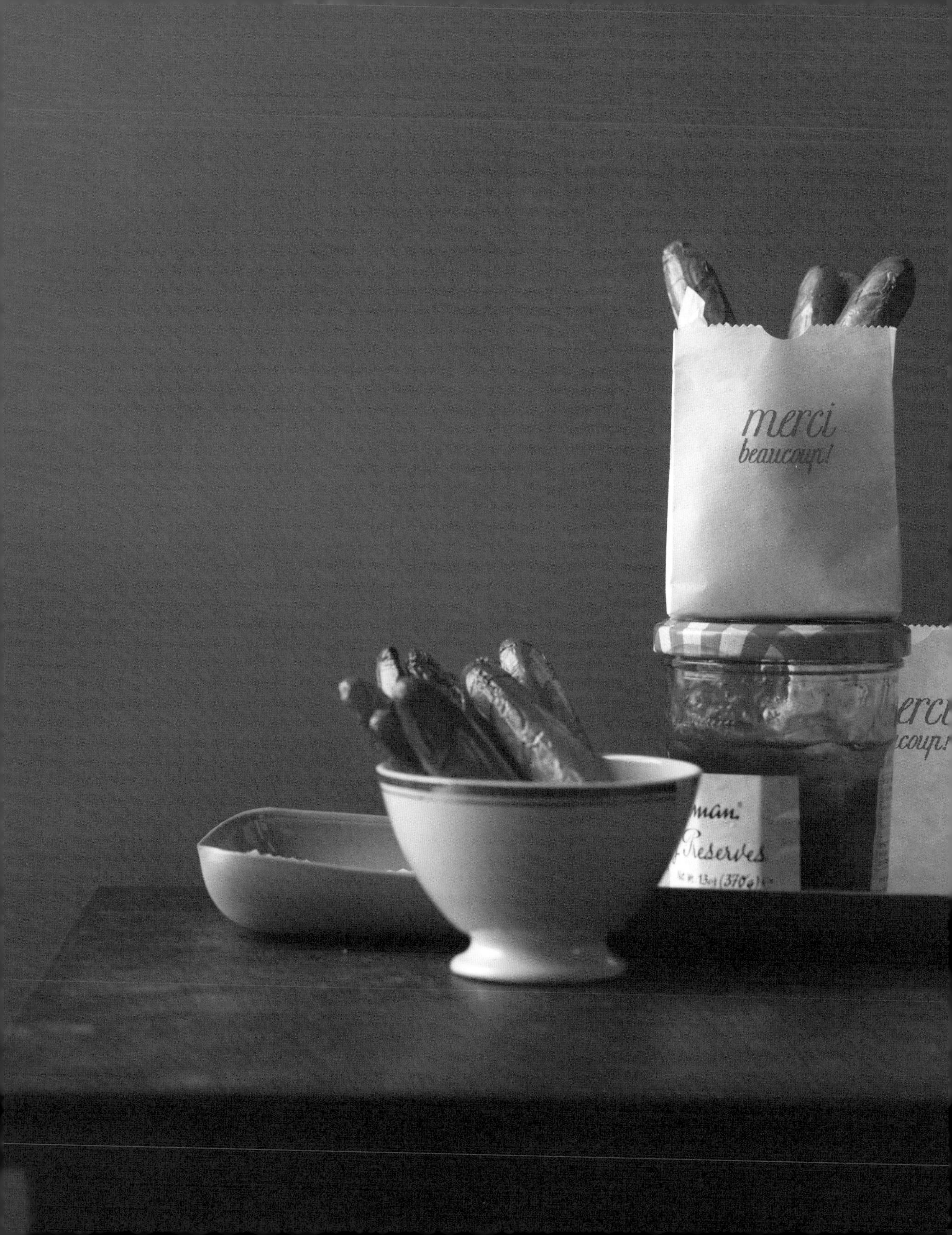
merci
beaucoup!

MINI GOODIE BAG

These goodie bags are a far cry from brown paper grocery bags. Crafting a bag from paper is simple to do and looks much better. Use these to wrap gifts, hold treats like cookies or crackers, or even to store small items on a shelf. Adding a personalized message on the front will make it extra-special.

Supplies

Goodie bag template

2 sheets 8½-by-11-in (22-by-28-cm) light- or medium-weight paper, such as scrapbooking paper, in desired color or pattern

Utility knife or scissors

Cutting mat

Bone folder

Ruler

Glue stick

Pinking scissors

Labels or rubber stamps, or use the Merci Beaucoup stamp template (optional)

Goodies (mandatory!)

Tissue paper (optional)

1 Prep the bag template.

Download the goodie bag template from www.chroniclebooks.com/papercraft, adjust to the size required, and print onto the back side of the light- or medium-weight paper. Using a utility knife, carefully cut out the template on a cutting mat (see Fig. 1). Using a bone folder and a ruler, score lightly along the lines on the back of the paper so they will fold more easily (see Fig. 2).

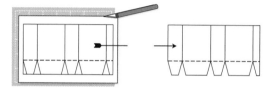

Fig. 1

Fig. 2

2 Construct the bag.

Fold down the flaps along the bottom edge of the bag. Glue the long side tab to form a bag shape (see Fig. 3).

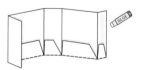

Fig. 3

3 **Form the base of the bag.**

Use a glue stick to secure the base of the bag, folding in the short end tabs first (see Fig. 4).

Fig. 4

4 **Finalize construction.**

Form the pleats down the sides of the bag by pressing the long edges together gently so that the paper is pushed inward (see Fig. 5).

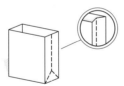

Fig. 5

Continued…

⑤ Add decorative elements.

Using scissors, cut a half oval shape in the center of the top edge to mimic a shopping-bag look (see Fig. 6). Use pinking scissors to cut across the top edge to finish the look (see Fig. 7).

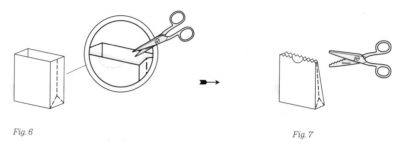

Fig. 6

Fig. 7

⑥ Finishing touches.

Embellish and customize your bag with labels or rubber stamps. Add goodies and finish it off by stuffing the bag with colorful tissue, if desired (see Fig. 8).

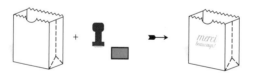

Fig. 8

Additional Ideas

....

Fold down the top, and seal with a pretty label.

....

Try different types of ribbons and strings or even a paper handle. These can be attached to the shorter sides of the bag.

When using ribbons or strings: Using a hole punch, make 2 holes, ½ in (13 mm) from the top edge of the short width of the bag. Thread an end of a 12-in (30.5-cm) string or ribbon from the inside out through one hole and back in the hole on the other side. Tie a knot in each ribbon end on the inside of the cone. This creates the handle.

For a paper handle: Using a utility knife and metal edge ruler, cut 2 strips of ¼-by-6-in (.5-by-15-cm) of the same white butcher paper used. Using a glue stick, attach one end of the paper strip to the wider side of the bag about ½ in (13 mm) from the edge of the bag. Take the remaining edge and, with a folding motion toward inside of the bag, attach the end to the other side of the bag. This will create an arch look to the handle. Repeat for the other side.

cone
WREATH

This cone wreath project brings a modern interpretation to the standard holiday wreath. This is the perfect opportunity to stretch your creative muscles and rethink the more obvious components and color schemes. You can use the center of the wreath to post a photo, a festive token, or a family crest or monogram. The paper ribbon banner is a great way to herald your season's wishes. You can easily customize this for any special event.

Supplies

22 sheets of 8½-by-11-in (22-by-28-cm) cover-weight paper in desired color

Double-sided tape

Glue dots (optional)

Scissors

Decorative-edge scissors (optional)

Pencil

10-in (25-cm) round plate or bowl

Cardboard

Hot glue gun

Banner template

1 sheet 11-by-17-in (28-by-43-cm) cover-weight paper in desired color for banner and center

Marker or felt-tip pen

6-in (15-cm) round plate or bowl

4-by-48-in (10-by-122-cm) ribbon (or longer as desired)

1 # Create the cones.

Lay a sheet of 8½-by-11-in (22-by-28-cm) cover-weight paper, colored-side down, on a work surface. Place a strip of double-sided tape along the entire length of one of the long sides. Twist the adjacent edge toward and past the tape strip, tightening as needed, and join, forming a cone shape. Gently press together to stick. The cone should be about 12 in (30 cm) tall (see Fig. 1). To make a 24-in (60-cm)-diameter wreath, continue until you have made 22 cones. Try using glue dots if the paper does not stick well enough.

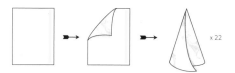

Fig. 1

2 # Clean up the cone edges.

Using scissors, trim the open end of each cone (see Fig. 2). Decorative-edge scissors can be used if you wish.

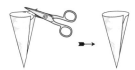

Fig. 2

❸ Form the wreath.

With a pencil, trace the edge of a round 10-in (25-cm)-diameter plate onto cardboard, and, using scissors, cut out the circle shape (see Fig. 3). (There's no need to make it a perfect circle, since it will be hidden.) With the points facing inward, distribute the cones evenly clockwise around the circle base. Once you have tested the fit of the cones in the wreath, remove all the cones. Apply a small dab of hot glue to the point of the first cone. Place the pointy part, seam-side down, in the center and repeat with the rest of the cones, one by one around the circle. Let dry (see Fig. 4).

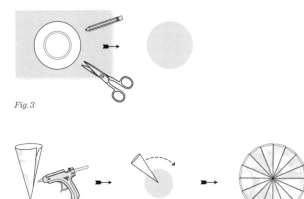

Fig. 3

Fig. 4

Continued...

④ Finishing touches.

Download the banner template from www.chroniclebooks.com/papercraft and print out on cover-weight paper to make the wreath banner and center. Using scissors, cut out the banner and add your own text with a marker. To add the wreath center, with a pencil trace the edge of a 6-in (15-cm)-diameter plate on a colored piece of cover-weight paper to create a circle. Cut out. Apply hot glue to the back of the circle and position it in the center of the wreath. Feel free to decorate the center before adhering it to the wreath (we covered ours with paper). Position the banner on the wreath and apply using the glue gun (see Fig. 5). Attach a loop of ribbon to the back of the large cardboard circle using the glue gun and hang the wreath from the ribbon (see Fig. 6).

Fig. 5

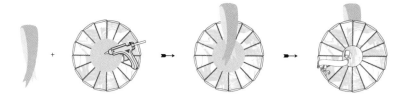

Fig. 6

Additional Ideas

....

The center of the wreath can be anything—
try monograms, numbers, pictures, or a pretty
pattern or illustration.

....

Print a blank banner template and write a
message of your own with a calligraphy pen.

....

Play with scale—a very small wreath can be
a darling accent!

MOMMY
and me
FLOWER
SHOES

Spend some quality time with your daughter making these adorable paper-flower shoes. These shoes are cute enough to make any feet dance, no matter how young or old your daughter might be. When you are done, you can wear your matching shoes out on the town. Of course, this doesn't have to be a mother/daughter craft—make them for yourself or as a gift.

Supplies

Pencil

Ruler

3 sheets 8-by-12-in (20-by-30-cm) tissue paper in colors coordinated with shoes

Scissors

Flower template

1 sheet 8½-by-11-in (22-by-28-cm) plain cover-weight paper for template

Japanese hole punch or sharp pen tip

⅛-in (3-mm)-diameter mini brads

Hot glue gun

Shoe clip

Shoes

① Prep the flower petal materials.

With a pencil and ruler, measure and mark fifteen 4-in (10-cm) squares from the tissue sheets. Cut out the squares with your scissors. Then, stack the sheets together in this manner: 6 sheets, 5 sheets, 3 sheets, and 1 sheet (see Fig. 1). Set aside. Download the flower template from www.chroniclebooks.com/papercraft and print out onto the plain coverweight paper and cut out the pieces with scissors.

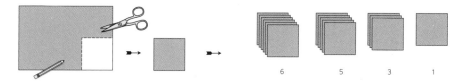

Fig. 1

② Create the flower petals.

With a pencil, draw the large flower shape template on the top sheet of the stack with 5 pieces. Draw the medium flower template on the stack with 6 sheets, the small flower template on the stack with 3 sheets, and the mini flower template on the single sheet. Using scissors, cut along the lines you have drawn (see Fig. 2). Keep the different stacks separate and set aside.

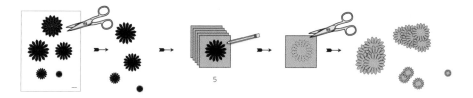

Fig. 2

③ Assemble all the parts.

Punch a small hole in the center of the flower on each stack using a Japanese hole punch. Place a mini brad in the center of the mini flower cutout. Put the stack of 3 small flowers on the brad behind the mini flower. Add the stack of 6 medium flowers, followed by the stack of 5 large flowers. Open up and bend apart the ends of the brad to keep the flowers secure. Open up the tissue sheets to make it look like an open flower. Rotate the petals to give the flower a full look (see Fig. 3).

Fig. 3

④ Finishing touches.

Using a hot glue gun, attach the flower to the shoe clip. Attach the clip to one of the shoes (see Fig. 4).

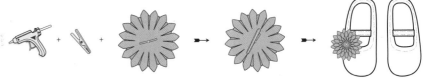

Fig. 4

Additional Ideas

These flowers can be worn anywhere—use one to accent your dress or put one on a hair clip.

Play with scale and shapes. Multiple tiny flower clusters can be adorable.

Tanner　THE BOOK OF BOND　Viking

★★

HENDRIK NICOLAAS WERKMAN OBRA IMPRESA 1923-1944

CONE ■ ROOTS & ROUTES / ART IN THE 20TH CENTURY ■ HORIZON

GREETINGS, DEARIE! Humor from Hallmark Contemporary Cards

WILLIE PHOTOGRAPHED BY KEN REGAN · WORDS BY MICHAEL MANN

sock monkeys

diane arbus　An Aperture Monograph

Anthony Blunt · Picasso · PICASS　New York Graphic Society

old-fashioned
paper
FRAME

As designers, we tend to be attracted to the feel of certain periods in history. These vintage-inspired paper frames bring to mind an era long since past and charm us in a way that manufactured picture frames can't. Play around with different template sizes and adjust the cutouts to fit the size of your photographs. For a different look, arrange the frames in shadow boxes with other small trinkets. These frames are a wonderful way to add some charm to your photo gallery. Best of all, they are a breeze to make.

Supplies

Frame templates

3 sheets 11-by-17-in
(28-by-43-cm) white text-
weight paper

Utility knife

Ruler

Cutting mat

Pencil

1 sheet 11-by-17-in
(28-by-43-cm) black
cover-weight paper

1 sheet 8½-by-11-in
(22-by-28-cm) text-weight
Kraft paper

1 sheet 8½-by-11-in
(22-by-28-cm) text-weight
newsprint

Japanese hole punch

Star hand punch

Glue stick

Photograph for frame

Transparent tape

Hole punch

Fabric ribbon, thin ribbon,
or string

① Create the frame.

Download the three frame templates from www.chroniclebooks.com/papercraft
and print onto the white text-weight paper. Using a utility knife and ruler, on a
cutting mat, carefully cut along the template lines (see Fig. 1). Then, with a pencil,
trace frame 1 onto the black paper, frame 2 onto the Kraft paper, and frame 3
onto the newsprint. Cut out the pieces (see Fig. 2).

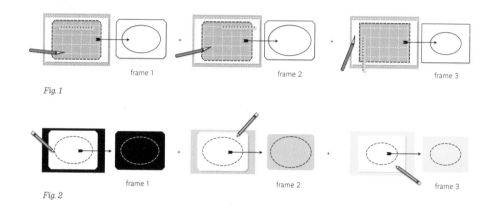

frame 1   frame 2   frame 3

Fig. 1

frame 1   frame 2   frame 3

Fig. 2

② Cut out the centers.

Using the utility knife on the cutting mat, carefully and cleanly cut out the oval
shapes from the middle of the frames. Discard the center cutouts (see Fig 3).

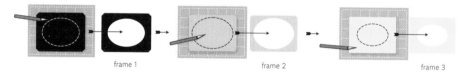

frame 1   frame 2   frame 3

Fig. 3

③ Decorate the frame.

Using the Japanese hole punch and the star hand punch, punch around the entire oval opening of the newsprint frame (see Fig. 4). When finished, apply glue with the glue stick all over the edges and place the newsprint frame behind the black frame. Center the Kraft frame on top of the black frame (see Fig. 5). Apply glue to the back of the Kraft paper frame and press and smooth out onto the black frame.

Fig. 4   Fig. 5

④ Add a photo.

With the frame facing down, place the photo facedown in the center, securing it with small amounts of transparent tape on each side (see Fig. 6).

Fig. 6

Continued...

⑤ Finishing touches.

Punch two holes in the top edge of the frame, 1 in (2.5 cm) down from the top and 1 in (2.5 cm) apart. Cut the ribbon to the desired length. If using a fabric ribbon, cut the ends of the ribbon into a forked shape. If using a thin ribbon or string, cut clean edges. Insert one end of the ribbon through one hole in the front and the other end through the other hole in the front. Center the ribbon so equal lengths extend from the back of the holes. Tie a bow or knot at the height where the frame is to be hung (see Fig. 7) and hang the frame.

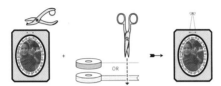

Fig. 7

Additional Ideas

Use labels to title the frame.

Play with different sizes to create a wall of paper frames.

These can make great gifts. Insert a favorite photo of yourself and your loved one. For an extra finishing touch, use glass and plate hangers to create a polished look.

Animal DRINK TAGS

Nobody likes losing their drink or picking up the wrong glass at a party. That's where these darling (and functional) drink tags come into play. They add a layer of character to any party and serve to keep everyone's drinks straight. You can get totally creative in coming up with your own thematic name tags, or use the provided animal templates (these work great for kids' parties, too). Your guests are sure to adore them.

Supplies

Animal templates
(koala, squirrel, giraffe,
octopus, elephant)

1 sheet 8½-by-11-in
(22-by-28-cm) black
cover-weight paper

Utility knife

Ruler

Cutting mat

Glasses in various sizes
and shapes

Swizzle sticks or straws

Double-sided tape

White or silver pen
or marker

① Cut out the animal shapes.

Download the animal templates you wish to use from www.chroniclebooks.com/
papercraft and print out onto the cover-weight paper. Using a utility knife and ruler,
carefully cut out the shapes on a cutting mat (see Fig. 1).

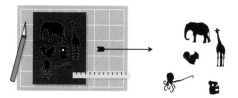

Fig. 1

② Coordinate the animals to the glasses.

Decide which animal will go with which type of glass or swizzle stick (see Fig. 2).

Fig. 2

③ Assemble the tags.

Figure out where the animals should be positioned. Place double-sided tape onto the back of each cut-out animal and adhere to a glass. If desired, with a white or silver pen, write a guest's name on each shape (see Fig. 3). A hot glue gun can also be used to attach the animal card onto a straw. Place two dots of glue on the straw and position the animal card, and press down lightly to adhere.

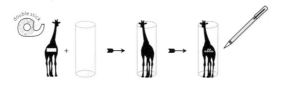

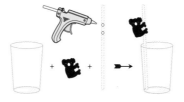

Fig. 3

Additional Ideas

These animals can be used to identify food platters as well. Place them on skewers and label each item.

PAPER
POCKET
square

This project is perfect for any true gentleman. It is a dapper accessory and is also functional—you can use it to jot down notes or contact information on, or even use it as a mini photo album. Truman constructed this pocket square for a friend's wedding. He put notes for his speech on one side and photos of himself and his friend on the reverse. Then, he presented it to his friend as a gift when he was done. The options for the design pattern are endless.

Ladies, this also makes a great little gift for the men in your life, for Father's Day, anniversaries, or just because.

Supplies

Pocket square template

One 8½-by-11-in
(22-by-28-cm) sheet
cover-weight paper

Utility knife

Ruler

Cutting mat

1 sheet 8½-by-11-in
(22-by-28-cm) patterned
paper (optional, if not
using template pattern)

1 sheet 11-by-17-in
(28-by-43-cm) text-weight
paper (for the inside of the
pocket square)

Pencil

Bone folder

Glue brush and adhesive
such as PVA glue

❶ Prep the pieces.

Download the pocket square template from www.chroniclebooks.com/papercraft
and print onto the cover-weight paper. There are two sizes to choose from. The
smaller 3¼-in (8-cm) size should fit most pockets. We suggest you measure your
pocket beforehand to make sure. Using a utility knife and ruler, carefully cut
out the shapes on a cutting mat. Or cut out two squares, each 3¼ by 3¼ in (8 by
8 cm), on patterned paper, if desired (see Fig. 1).

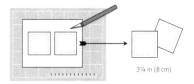

3¼ in (8 cm)

Fig. 1

❷ Construct the inside pages.

Cut a rectangle 3⅛ by 12½ in (7 by 32 cm) from the text-weight paper (see Fig. 2).
With a pencil, measure and draw a vertical line 3⅛ in (7 cm) from the left edge of
the rectangle. Using a bone folder and the ruler, fold along the 3⅛-in (7 cm) mark.
Continue folding the same measurement back and forth until you have folded your
entire strip like an accordion (see Fig. 3).

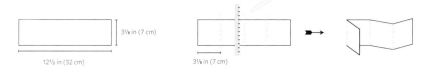

3⅛ in (7 cm)

12½ in (32 cm)

3⅛ in (7 cm)

Fig. 2   *Fig. 3*

③ Assemble the pocket square.

Using the glue brush and adhesive, lightly apply glue to one end of the accordion panel. Place it in the center of one of the cover squares that you cut in step 1. Repeat with the other side of the accordion (see Fig. 4).

Fig. 4

Additional Ideas

Add additional accordion folds for more writing room.

Before gluing, insert a ribbon between the cover panel and accordion panel on each end, and tie the ribbons together to close.

Experiment with different covers. It can be fun to print a full-bleed photo to use as a cover. Print out the photo on cover-weight paper and follow the cover-making instructions above. To turn this into a mini photo album, print photos onto photo paper and put one on each of the panels.

PAPER BOOK cover

Back in the '80s, we were walking around high school with textbooks covered in paper grocery bags with "Van Halen," "AC/DC," and "I Luv Simon Le Bon" scribbled across them and rips running up the seams. We have gotten more creative with our book covers since then, using more attractive patterns and antique designs. These days, we use paper book covers to brighten up our library and organize old, mismatched journals and notebooks by grouping by year or subject. You also can use this DIY project in place of wrapping a book as a gift.

Another great idea is to use this craft to customize a wedding guest book. It is a wonderful way to upgrade the generic types of guest books you normally find at your local stationery store.

Supplies

Photocopier

Vintage pattern or image, such as clip-art patterns, found patterns, wrapping paper, or wallpaper

Large sheet of text-weight paper, three times the width of the book to be covered

Pencil

Ruler

Scissors or utility knife (optional)

Bone folder (optional)

Label or rubber stamps (optional)

❶ Create the pattern sheet.

Photocopy your chosen pattern at a local copy shop onto text-weight paper using a monochrome setting. Experiment by selecting different color options. You can adjust the percentage of color saturation to get lighter or darker patterns. If covering a large book, ask the store to print it on an oversized printer (see Fig. 1). Keep in mind that the longer edges of the paper should be three times the width of the book and there should be at least 4 in (10 cm) extra on the height of the book for proper coverage.

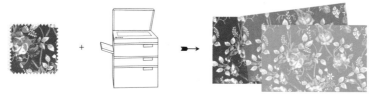

Fig. 1

❷ Measure and prep the cover.

Place the text-weight paper facedown on a work surface. Center the book on the paper. Using a pencil and ruler, draw a horizontal line along the top and bottom edges of the book. Remove the book and fold the paper in at the drawn lines (see Fig. 2). Trim with scissors if the paper is too large.

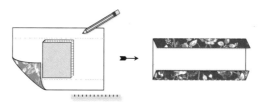

Fig. 2

③ Construct the cover.

Place the book back on the paper, centered horizontally. Open the front cover of the book, and fold the left edge in. For a clean crisp fold, try using a bone folder. Close the book, keeping the left edge folded tightly in place and the paper wrapped tightly around. Open the back cover, and fold the right edge in. Slide each of the covers into the paper flaps, one side at a time (see Fig. 3).

Fig. 3

④ Finishing touches.

Add a label or rubber-stamped title to the cover of the book, if desired (see Fig. 4).

Fig. 4

Additional Ideas

Use for a guest book by covering a lined journal and adding a ribbon to the spine. The ribbon should be attached with a piece of tape to the spine of the journal prior to wrapping the cover.

Use various papers, such as wallpaper, wrapping paper, butcher paper, or the old-school cut-up shopping bag.

Mustache DRINK TOPPERS

This idea was inspired by a Christmas holiday visit to California a few years ago. We came across some gag mustache toys at an old vintage shop in New York, and thought it would be fun to wear them for our holiday get-together. We have a large family and decided that when it came time to exchange gifts, everyone had to choose a mustache to wear and pose for a witty photo before opening a gift. Our families had a blast, and we reinterpreted this idea into our Mustache Drink Toppers. It's fun to play disguises, and children and adults alike are always amused with this lighthearted quip. We also discovered that these are a certified, guaranteed cure for the common case of camera shyness.

Supplies

Mustache template

1 sheet 8½-by-11-in
(22-by-28-cm) white
text-weight paper

Scissors

1 sheet 8½-by-11-in
(22-by-28-cm) construc-
tion paper in black,
red, orange, gray, or brown

Pencil

Hole punch in the same
width as the straws

Bendable or straight straws

Hot glue gun (optional)

Drinking glasses

❶ Make the mustache template.

Download the mustache template from www.chroniclebooks.com/papercraft and print onto text-weight paper. Using scissors, carefully cut out the template (see Fig. 1).

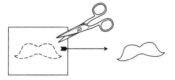

Fig. 1

❷ Create the mustaches.

Place a mustache piece onto the colored paper and trace the shape with a pencil. Repeat for as many mustaches as you want. Using scissors, cut out the shapes (see Fig. 2).

Fig. 2

③ Assemble the straws.

Using the hole punch, punch a hole in the center of each mustache and insert a straw. The mustache should be sitting right above the bend (see Fig. 3). *Note*: If not using a bendable straw, do not punch a hole in the middle of the mustache; instead, use a hot glue gun to attach the mustache to the front of the straight straw (see Fig. 3a).

OR

Fig. 3   *Fig. 3a*

④ Finishing touches.

Pour a cool beverage into the glasses, add the straws, and enjoy (see Fig. 4).

Fig. 4

Additional Ideas

Use different colored paper to match guests' hair color.

Put a mustache on a stick to use as a masquerade or for taking fun pictures.

Make a mustache napkin ring by attaching it to a ribbon or paper band.

Bumble-BEE POP-UP CARD

The earliest historical examples of pop-ups date as far back as the thirteenth century. It is a testament to the ingenuity of the pop-up card that we are still enamored with it so many centuries later. A handmade card is always a pleasant surprise—a handmade pop-up card is downright impressive. A pop-up seems delicate and intricate, but the good news is that assembling one is not complicated at all. We provided a basic template for this project, but there is lots of room for variation. So get creative!

Supplies

Pop-up template

1 sheet 8½-by-11-in (22-by-28-cm) white cover-weight paper

Utility knife

Cutting mat

Colored pencils, markers or crayons

One 5-by-7-in (12-by-17-cm) folded blank greeting card

Glue stick or double-sided tape

Pen

One 5⅛-by-7⅛-in (13-by-18-cm) A7 envelope

1 Print the template.

Download the pop-up template from www.chroniclebooks.com/papercraft and print onto the cover-weight paper. With a utility knife and ruler, carefully cut out the pieces on a cutting mat. Note that each bee has a corresponding rectangle; they are both numbered the same. Keep them together. Color in the bee cutouts with colored pencils (see Fig. 1).

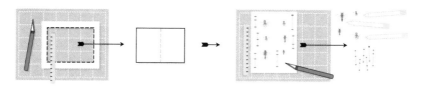

Fig. 1

2 Make the step formation.

Fold a rectangle piece from the template along the dotted lines. Open up the piece. You should see three scored marks. Arrange to create a step formation (see Fig. 2). Open the folded greeting card 90 degrees. Test out your rectangle steps in the card: Position the steps so the little legs are flush against the top and bottom of the card, and test by closing the card (see Fig. 3). The card and the step pieces should close and open without disrupting each of the pieces. No other folds or creases should be made. These steps will be attached to the card along with the printed bees.

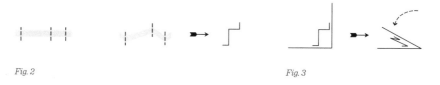

Fig. 2   *Fig. 3*

3 Assemble the card elements with the steps.

Collect all the rectangle steps and bee cutouts and arrange them in the order given on the template. Adhere the bees to the front of their matching steps (see Fig. 4). Apply glue to the back of the bee you want to put in the center of the card and attach it to the front of the center step, near the bend in the step. Test the pop-up function by closing the card and reopening it to see how it performs (see Fig. 5). Move the bee if necessary. Repeat with the other cutouts, so the bees are arranged in an attractive way on the fronts of the steps and on the card itself (see Fig. 6).

Apply glue to the back sides of the short ends of the steps and adhere them onto the card in the same manner as was tested in step 2.

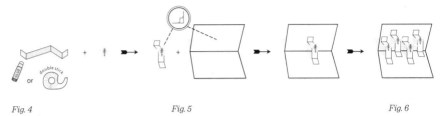

Fig. 4   *Fig. 5*   *Fig. 6*

---

4 Finishing touches.

Use a pen to write a message on the card and insert the card in the envelope (see Fig. 7).

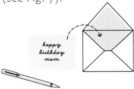

Fig. 7

Additional Ideas

This method can be used for any cutouts. Play with the scale and length of the steps and layer on cutouts throughout the card. Any size card and envelope will work. Play and have fun!

Try letters for a pop-up message, or cutout photos.

Make your own pop-up storybook! Draw out your story and decide on what pop-up pieces you want to focus on. Follow the basic process but keep in mind that the pop-up element works only when things are placed toward the center of the crease.

Beehive
GARDEN
stakes

These charming Beehive Garden Stakes make a great gift for any avid green thumb and might even motivate an aspiring gardener as well. Even if gardening isn't your favorite pastime, these beehives can be a sweet addition to a planted pot or small herb garden. Their simplicity means no degree in horticulture is necessary. Time to get bzzzzz-y!

Supplies

Beehive and banner templates

1 sheet 8½-by-11-in (22-by-28-cm) each yellow and black construction or cover-weight paper

1 sheet 8½-by-11-in (22-by-28-cm) cream construction or cover-weight paper

1 sheet 8½-by-11-in (22-by-28-cm) white text-weight paper

Utility knife

Cutting mat

Pencil

Scissors

Glue stick

2 wooden craft sticks or skewers

Pinking scissors (optional)

White-ink gel pen

① Print the templates and cut out the pieces.

Download the beehive template from www.chroniclebooks.com/papercraft and print two of each beehive shape onto the yellow cover-weight paper. (You can substitute the cream or white paper if you wish to just use the printout directly as the actual pieces.) Print the banner template on text paper. You will end up with two different beehive sets and one banner shape. Using a utility knife, carefully cut out the pieces on a cutting mat. With a pencil, trace the beehives onto the cream cover-weight paper and the banner onto the black cover-weight paper. Repeat so you have one banner for each garden stake. Cut out the pieces (see Fig. 1).

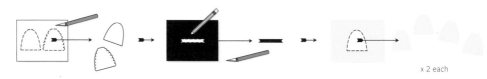

x 2 each

Fig. 1

② Make the beehive openings.

Using scissors, cut 2 small arch shapes, each with a straight bottom, from the black cover-weight paper, for the beehive openings. Apply glue to the back of each black arch, and adhere each to the bottom of a beehive front, with the straight edges flush (see Fig. 2).

Fig. 2

③ Assemble the beehives.

Flip over a beehive front and apply glue to the back of it. Lay a craft stick atop the glue-covered beehive, perpendicular to the bottom edge, so that about 1 in (2.5 cm) of the stick is on the beehive and the rest extends out. Align the beehive back with the beehive front and press to adhere. The stick should now be securely in place between the paper sheets (see Fig. 3). Repeat with the other hive.

Fig. 3

④ Finishing touches.

Try using pinking scissors on the edge of the banner for a different edge. Using the white-ink pen, write the plant or herb names on the black banners. Using a utility knife, cut the craft stick or skewer to the length you want. Apply glue to each stake about ½ in (13 mm) below the hive and press the banner on to adhere (see Fig. 4). Place the garden stakes into soil near the plants they will identify.

Fig. 4

Additional Ideas

These also make adorable food labels. Follow the same directions above, but place the labels in cheese platters or appetizer trays.

Use them as gift labels if giving plants or baked goods.

Make them small and use as cupcake toppers.

Recipe BOOK

We very much enjoy cooking but haven't always been organized about it. A testament to this fact is the sad state of our recipe collection, which consists of scraps of stationery, odd-sized index cards, and crumpled magazine cutouts. All the recipes are jumbled up and carelessly thrown into a drawer, and get covered with oil splatters and food stains whenever we use them. This recipe book was exactly what we needed. It has a clean design that looks nice on the kitchen counter and keeps all of our different recipes neatly stored in one place.

Supplies

Spine title template

Pattern texture
template

Recipe card template

Tab template

Clip-art images

3 sheets 8½-by-11-in
(22-by-28-cm) text-weight
paper

3 sheets white cover-weight
paper, at least one at 12 in
(30.5 cm) square

One 8½-by-11-in
(22-by-28-cm) sheet of
2-by-1-in (5-by-2.5-cm)
adhesive labels

Scissors or paper cutter

3-hole punch (or handheld
single-hole punch)

Pen

Glue stick

3-ring binder (1 in [2.5 cm]
wide)

Plastic sheet protectors
for 3-ring binder (full-size
sheets and sheets sized to
hold two photos, each 4 by
6 in [10 by 15 cm])

❶ Download the templates.

Download the spine title, pattern texture, recipe card, and tab templates from www.chroniclebooks.com/papercraft (you can use one of the general spine titles we have provided on the site, such as "Breakfast," "Lunch," "Dinner," and "Dessert," or customize your title in the Word document by substituting your own). Also download any clip-art images you wish to use. Print the title you need onto the text-weight paper. Use the provided pattern template or your own paper. Print the recipe cards onto the cover-weight paper. Print the tab template onto a sheet of labels. Print the clip-art images onto text-weight paper.

❷ Create the binder spine title.

Using scissors, cut out the spine title, recipe cards, and clip-art images. Set aside (see Fig. 1).

recipe cards

Fig. 1

❸ Make the binder dividers.

Using scissors, cut the cover-weight paper to 9¼ by 11 in (23.5 by 28 cm). Using the 3-hole punch, make holes along the left side where the paper will be inserted into the 3-ring binder (see Fig. 2). Repeat for each divider you wish to use.

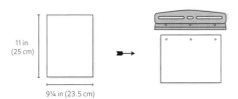

11 in
(25 cm)

9¼ in (23.5 cm)

Fig. 2

④ Make the divider tabs.

Remove the divider tabs from the sheet of labels, and attach them to the binder dividers: Affix one end of a label to the top of a divider, near the right-hand corner. Fold the label in half and press to adhere to the other side of the divider. Label tabs as needed with a pen. Repeat with the next label and divider, staggering the labels as you go, so that when the dividers are stacked you can see each tab (see Fig. 3).

Fig. 3

⑤ Assemble the binder.

Using scissors, cut a sheet of cover-weight paper to 9¾ by 11¼ in (25 by 30 cm) for the cover. Decorate the spine and cover by adhering the clip-art cutouts with a glue stick. Slip the spine and cover labels inside the clear plastic on the side and front of the binder (see Fig. 4).

Fig. 4

Continued…

6 **Finishing touches.**

Put the dividers into the rings in the binder, and put a few sheet protectors after each divider. You can add on as you increase your recipe collection. Write your recipes on the recipe cards and insert them into the plastic sleeves. Put a few blank recipe cards in the pockets at the back for future use (see Fig. 5). Now you're ready to get cooking!

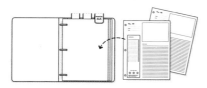

Fig. 5

Additional Ideas

Follow these instructions to create an
organizational binder for any use, such as
work projects or household information.
Make binders to organize your finances,
important documents, home renovation notes,
and so on.

TISSUE
STARS AND
MOON

Children love attaching glow-in-the-dark stars to the ceilings over their beds. Why not add another dimension with this hanging moon and stars? This project is a fun and easy way to decorate a nursery or a child's room to inspire little minds to think big. It's another alternative to the conventional mobile, and because these celestial bodies are made out of lightweight tissue paper, they are safe enough to hang over a crib or bed. We all encourage children to reach for the stars—why not give them actual stars? These make fun party decorations as well.

Supplies

4 sheets 20-by-30-in
(51-by-76-cm) silver matte
tissue paper

Ruler

Scissors

2 sheets 20-by-30-in
(51-by-76-cm) silver
metallic tissue paper

Floral wire

Wire cutters

Monofilament or
fishing string

Ceiling hanging hooks

❶ Prepare the tissue.

Stack the 4 sheets of silver matte tissue and, using a ruler and scissors, cut into 9-by-12-in (21-by-30.5-cm) rectangles. Layer the 2 sheets of silver metallic tissue, and cut into 5-by-6-in (13-by-15-cm) rectangles. Combine the matte tissue so 8 rectangles are stacked together, and fold in 1¼-in (3-cm) accordion folds. Stack 4 rectangles of the metallic tissue and fold in 1-in (2.5-cm) accordion folds (see Fig. 1). Make as many of the silver metallic ones as you like. (We made five.)

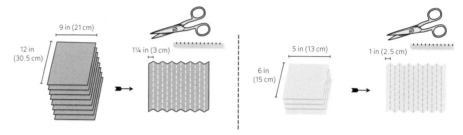

Fig. 1

❷ Form the stars and moon.

Trim the short edges of the metallic folded tissue to make a pointy shape, and round the edges of the matte folded tissue. Fold pieces of floral wire in half and wrap loosely around the centers of each of the folded tissue bundles. Twist around to secure and trim with wire cutters (see Fig. 2). Cut monofilament long enough to hang from the ceiling and loop around the center of the floral wire holding the tissue together (see Fig. 3).

Fig. 2

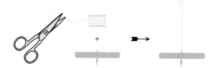

Fig. 3

Carefully separate all the orb layers, pulling each layer away from the center one at a time. Repeat until they form ball-like shapes (see Fig. 4).

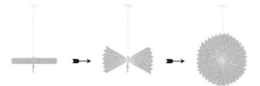

Fig. 4

---

③ Finishing touches.

Hang over a crib or seating area using ceiling hanging hooks (see Fig. 5).

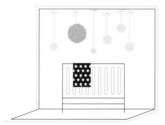

Fig. 5

Additional Ideas

....

Create a tissue-ball solar system using sizes and colors that mimic the various planets.

....

Hang over your dining area for party decorations.

woven CONE BASKET

This darling woven cone basket can be used for almost anything, such as for presenting a loved one with baked goods, or even to replace a traditional flower girl's basket at a wedding ceremony. You can use the basket to store small trinkets, to display flowers, or as a creative basket for party favors. Aside from its functionality, it has a lovely handmade look. Try customizing the basket with different colored patterns and adjust the proportions to fit your needs.

Supplies

2 sheets 8½-by-11-in (22-by-28-cm) cover-weight paper, each in a different color

Utility knife

Ruler

Cutting mat

Clear packing tape

Double-sided tape

Scissors or decorative-edge scissors (optional)

Hole punch

24 in of 4-mm rayon twist cord or ¼-in ribbon for handle

6-by-18-in (15-by-46-cm) ribbon

① Prep the materials.

Take one sheet of colored cover-weight paper and, using a utility knife and ruler on a cutting mat, carefully cut ½-in (13 mm)-wide strips lengthwise, stopping ½ in (13 mm) from the edge. Repeat with the other sheet of colored paper, rotating the paper and cutting along the shorter side so it goes crosswise (see Fig. 1).

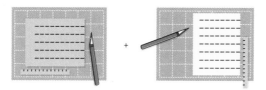

Fig. 1

② Weave the sheets.

Weave one strip in one sheet over and under the strips in the other sheet. Weave the next strip in the sheet under and over the strips in the other sheet. Repeat, alternating, until all strips are interwoven (see Fig. 2). When finished, tape down the edges with clear packing tape (see Fig. 3). Using a utility knife and ruler, clean up the edges to form a rectangle (see Fig. 4).

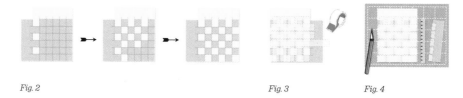

Fig. 2   *Fig. 3*   *Fig. 4*

③ Construct the cone shape.

Lay the paper on the table. Place double-sided tape along the entire length of one short side (see Fig. 5). Twist the adjacent edge toward and past the tape strip, tightening as needed, and join, forming a cone shape (see Fig. 6).

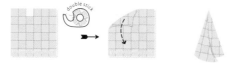

Fig. 5   *Fig. 6*

④ Trim the cone.

Using scissors, trim the wide end of the cone. Decorative-edge scissors can be used if you like (see Fig. 7).

OR

Fig. 7

⑤ Add ribbon handles.

Using a hole punch, make one hole, ½ in (13 mm) from the top edge. Repeat on the opposite side. Thread an end of the ribbon from the inside out through one hole and back in the hole on the other side. Tie a knot in each ribbon end on the inside of the cone. This creates the loop handle (see Fig. 8).

Fig. 8

Additional Ideas

Don't have time to weave? Skip the weaving instructions and go directly to making the cone out of plain paper. Quick and easy, but still very cute!

Decorate your own paper with rubber stamps and stencils prior to constructing the cone. This would be a fun craft project to do with your child.

Flip the cone upside down and it becomes a cone hat!

transparent WINDOW SHADE

Our design studio is in a quaint second-floor space with a large floor-to-ceiling window that looks out onto a lovely neighborhood in Manhattan. We try not to keep the curtains closed during business hours, so we needed something to give us just a little bit of privacy from the outside world, while still letting in natural light. These window shades were the perfect solution because they are easy to make and can quickly be switched out or removed. Since they are made of paper, they also can double as convenient backdrops to display artwork. This is a simple way to dress up your window.

Supplies

Measuring tape

Utility knife

Ruler

Cutting mat

Per window, 1 sheet clear vellum paper roll or large sheet at least the width of the window being covered

Rubber stamp

Ink stamp pad in desired shade

Double-sided tape

Extension rod used to hang shade

Clear plastic rod

① Prepare the shade.

With measuring tape, measure the width and height of the window you're covering. Using a utility knife and ruler with a cutting mat, carefully cut the vellum so it is 1 in (2.5 cm) narrower than the window width and 2 in (5 cm) longer than the window height (see Fig. 1).

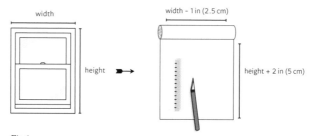

Fig. 1

② Create the pattern.

Select a rubber stamp pattern of your choice. We used a custom-made stamp (see Fig. 2). Using the rubber stamp and ink stamp pad (we used red ink), stamp on the artwork in the pattern you desire and let dry (see Fig. 3).

Fig. 2

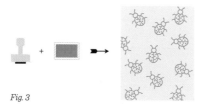

Fig. 3

③ Hang the shade.

Flip the vellum over to the back side and apply double-sided tape along the top edge of the paper and gently fold in, enclosing the curtain rod extension in between. Attach the rod to the top of the window frame (see Fig. 4). Do the same to the opposite end of the shade and insert the clear rod. This will add some weight to the edge and keep the paper in place.

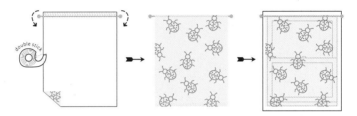

Fig. 4

Additional Ideas

Using paper punches adds texture and takes seconds to do—try it on the edges.

Stencils are great for more adventurous and crafty folks.

Gocco is a quick and easy way to create a silk-screen effect.

For an extra touch, stitch a line through the top where the paper folds into the rod, and at the bottom of the shade.

Use colored transparent vellum.

TURTLE-DOVE *ornaments*

Homemade ornaments bring sentiment and tradition to any holiday and make lovely gifts as well. The turtledove represents peace, so hang this ornament anywhere in your home to symbolize peace during the holiday season. As the holidays come and go, the doves will take on a mottled appearance, which will only add to their charm and signify the passing of the years.

Supplies

Dove ornament
template

1 sheet 8½-by-11-in
(22-by-28-cm) white
cover-weight paper

Utility knife

Cutting mat

Pencil

1 sheet 8½-by-11-in
(22-by-28-cm) cover-
weight paper in desired
color or pattern
(optional)

Glue stick

Japanese hole punch or
needle

Thin ribbon or
ornament-hanging wire

Scissors

① Prep the dove ornament templates.

Download the dove ornament template from www.chroniclebooks.com/papercraft
and print onto white cover-weight paper. Using a utility knife, carefully cut out
the pieces on a cutting mat (see Fig. 1). These will be the pieces of your ornament.
If you choose to use a color for your doves, these will be your template. Using a
pencil and utility knife, trace and cut out the shapes on colored paper if you choose
not to keep the doves white.

Fig. 1

② Make the dove ornaments.

Apply glue to the edge of the wings and apply to the matching bird bodies. Create a
crease near the edge to make a 3-D fold. The wing should stick out. You can have fun
here and play with different wing directions (see Fig. 2). Repeat for the second bird.

Fig. 2

③ Finalize the birds.

Using a Japanese hole punch, make a hole for the eye of each dove. Also make a small hole toward the center top of the body and thread a thin ribbon through the hole. A fun variation is to make a small envelope and glue it to one of the bird's beaks (template provided); (see Fig. 3).

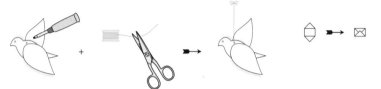

Fig. 3

④ Finishing touches.

Hang the doves on a garland, tree, or wreath (see Fig. 4).

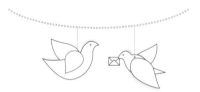

Fig. 4

Additional Ideas

Use these as gift tags.

Create an ornament garland—follow the directions from the flag banner project.

Create a paper wreath with these ornaments, and have each family member sign one. Put the holiday year in the center.

MATERIALS,

tools & RESOURCES

MATERIALS

ADHESIVES

There are different types of glue to suit the content and weight of the materials being used.

Craft glue
Also known as white glue, a water-based adhesive that dries clear.

Double-sided tape
Comes in rolls with two sticky sides. Peel off one side and place it on your paper, then remove the other side for adhering to another surface.

Glue dots
Available in rolls or sheets, these can be used to give a three-dimensional effect. They can also substitute for hot glue.

Glue stick
A solid form of glue that comes in a twist or push-up tube. Dries clear and doesn't wrinkle or overwet the paper. Great for using on tissue or crepe paper.

Hot glue
Comes in a solid stick form that is used with a glue gun. When it melts, the plastic glue sticks and cools as it dries. Great for when you need something a little more tacky and stronger than craft glue.

Mod Podge
White paste like glue that dries clear. Comes in matte or glossy finish.

PVA glue
An archival white, water-based glue. Most commonly used in bookbinding and print making.

PAPER

Paper is described in several different ways—by point sizes and by weight. The most common method is the pound weight, or GSM (grams per square meter). In this book, we refer to the pound weight (example: 80-pound cover).

Chipboard

Usually made from recycled paper, chipboard is a very thick, stiff board used in bookbinding and other projects that require a stiff backing. Sold at most art stores, it can also be found in the back of notebooks and business forms.

Cover-weight paper

This is a thick paper stock that comes in various weights. Generally, anything from 80- to 140-pound paper is considered to be cover stock or card stock. The best weight to run through a home inkjet printer is about 80-pound paper, and, for crafting, 110-pound paper.

Crepe paper

A tissue paper that has been coated with sizing and then "creped" to create the tiny gathers, crepe paper is often found in the form of party streamers. It has an elastic feel and is very pliable.

Text-weight paper

A lighter-weight and thinner paper stock than cover stock. Normal copy paper or writing paper is text-weight paper. These papers come in different finishes such as woven, linen, and smooth.

Tissue paper

The thinnest-weight paper and the most fragile. This paper is used most commonly in gift wrapping and comes in a wide variety of colors.

Tracing paper

Translucent paper that you can use to transfer an image to another paper surface. It can also be used to overlay one image on top of another to create different layers. This can be useful when you have artwork that you do not want to alter just yet.

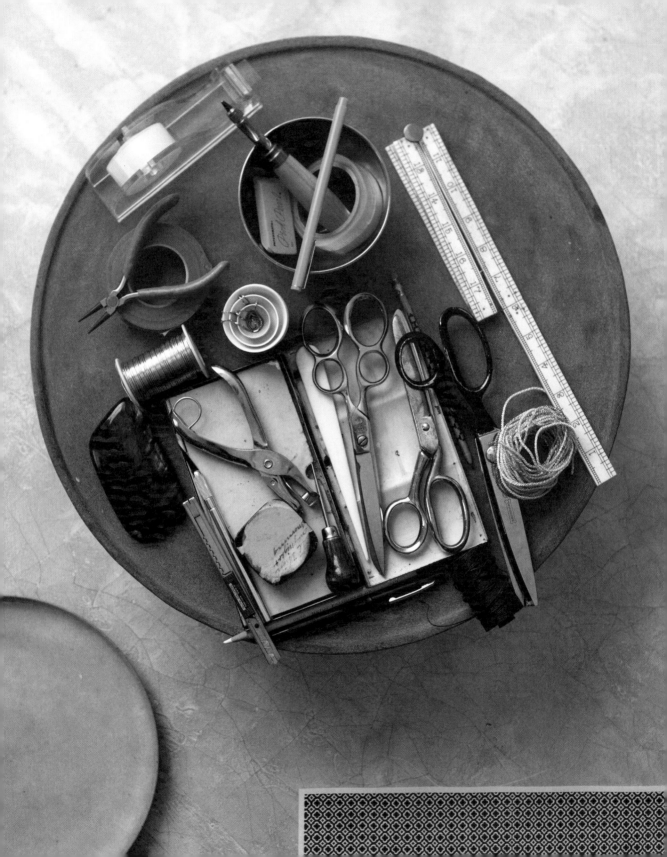

tools

Bone folder

A tool used to create smooth folds and creases. Typically shaped like a wooden tongue depressor, with a round or pointy end for working into corners.

Clip art

Copyright-free artwork and letters that can be reused (see Resources).

Cutting mat

A surface used to protect your table top when cutting materials with a utility knife. The mat has a ruled grid for making quick measurements and right angles.

Decorative paper punch

Available in various shapes and sizes. Works like a hole punch to create assorted shapes.

Gocco

A self-contained compact color printing system that is a quick and easy alternative to silk-screening. Minimal setup and cleanup required.

Hole punch

A tool that creates holes in sheets of paper.

Japanese hole punch

Unlike the restrictions of a plier-style hole punch, this tool allows you to punch a hole anywhere on the page. Comes with various bit sizes and can punch through several sheets of paper at once.

Metal ruler

Best used for a sharp and crisp edge when cutting with a utility knife. Available in various lengths.

Right-angle ruler

Looks like a triangle; used to create right angles.

Utility knife

A handheld tool containing small, replaceable razor blades for cutting materials. It is usually shaped like a pen, with a small, sharp blade that is excellent for making neat, accurate cuts.

RESOURCES

Art

Clipart: www.clipart.com
Dover Publications: www.doverpublications.com
iStockphoto (stock photos and vector illustrations): www.istock.com
My Fonts: www.myfonts.com
Veer (fonts and illustrations): www.veer.com

Decorations and Specialty Supplies

Create for Less (brads, adhesives, paper): www.createforless.com
Impress Rubber Stamps (rubber stamps, inks, tools, punches):
    www.impressrubberstamps.com
M&J Trimming (specialty ribbon and trims, buttons, and clasps): www.mjtrim.com
Oriental Trading Company (crafting and scrapbooking supplies):
    www.orientaltrading.com
Papermart (ribbon, tissue, boxes, and other paper supplies): www.papermart.com
Stampworx 2000 (custom rubber stamps): www.stampworx2000.biz
Tinsel Trading Company: www.tinseltrading.com

Fabrics

Hancock Fabrics: www.hancockfabrics.com
Joann Fabric and Craft Store: www.joann.com
Mood Fabrics: www.moodfabrics.com
Purl: www.purlsoho.com

Floral Supplies

Afloral: www.afloral.com
Jamali Garden Supplies: www.jamaligarden.com
Save on Crafts: www.save-on-crafts.com

General Art Materials and Supplies
Al Friedman: www.alfriedman.com
Dick Blick Art Materials: www.dickblick.com
Metalliferous (crafting tools, pliers, clippers, wires, rods): www.metalliferous.com
Michaels: www.michaels.com
Paper Presentation: www.paperpresentation.com
Paper Source: www.papersource.com
Pearl: www.pearlpaint.com
Print Icon: www.printicon.com
Utrecht Art Supplies: www.utrechtart.com

Paper
Apec: www.apecenvelopes.com
Apec-French Paper Company: www.mrfrench.com
Castle in the Air: www.castleintheair.biz
Envelope Mall: www.envelopemall.com
New York Central Art Supply (for printmaking, handmade papers):
    www.nycentralart.com
Paper Presentation: www.paperpresentation.com
Print Icon: www.printicon.com

Wallpaper
Jill Malek: www.jillmalek.com
Madison & Grow: www.madisonandgrow.com
Pattern Tales (modern and custom wallpaper): www.patterntales.com
Secondhand Rose (vintage wallpaper): www.secondhandrose.com

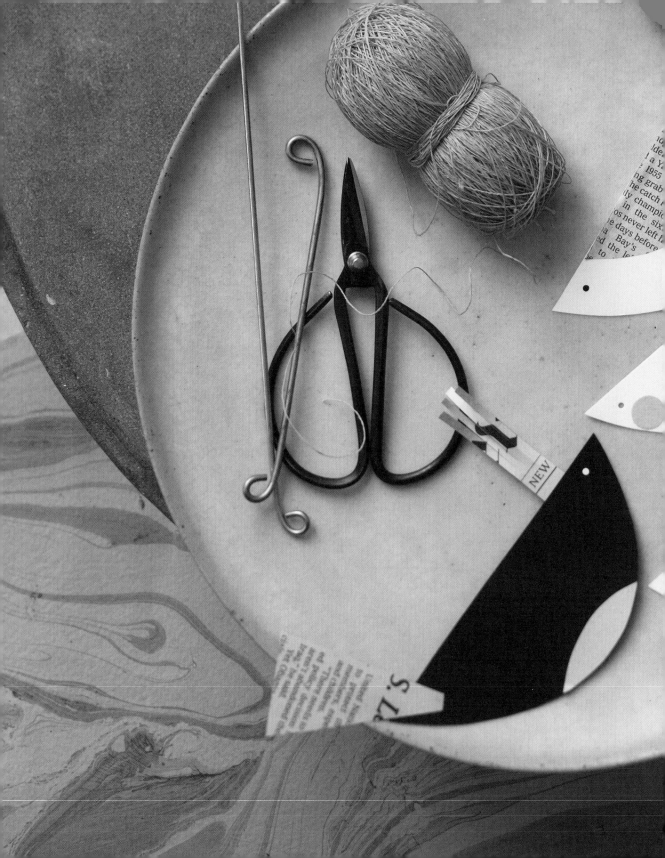

Acknowledgments

SPECIAL THANKS

We are so fortunate to have had the opportunity to work with such an amazing team. This book would not have been possible without all of you! We would like to take a moment to thank: Our wonderful editors at Chronicle, Jodi Warsaw and Laura Lee Mattingly. Thank you for the opportunity to make this project happen. Amy Su for her expert crafting and tireless attention to all of the tiniest details. Ann MacDonald for her extreme graciousness and generosity. Shirley Hong for keeping us fed with all of her culinary acumen. Our agent Melissa Flashman. Rae Nicoletti, Omotomi Omololu Lange, Naomi Demañana, Rachel Krauskopf, and Jesse Lawson for hair and makeup. The following Brooklyn shops for their generous loans: Adobe Home and Pomme. Thanks also to Aesthetic Movement for providing us with amazing pieces from the lines they represent: Roost, Wild & Wolf, Yellow Owl Workshop, Teroforma, and Mud Australia. Jacob Harris and Marisa Sellitti for all of the patience and support only the most loving spouses can give. John Francis Miller, for his brilliant modeling debut, and Olive Harris, the envy of canine models across the world. Johnny Miller for the beautiful photography and his lovely assistant Emily Roemer. And, of course, our most talented stylist who brought our projects to life, Randi Brookman Harris.